THE MYTH OF THE ARYAN INVASION OF INDIA

The Myth
of
The Aryan Invasion of India

David Frawley
(Vamadeva Shastri)

VOICE OF INDIA
New Delhi

ISBN 81-85990-20-4

© DAVID FRAWLEY

First Published: 1994
First Reprint: January 1995
Second Reprint: August 1998

Published by Voice of India, 2/18, Ansari Road, New Delhi – 110 002
and printed at Rajkamal Electric Press, Delhi – 110 033

CONTENTS

CONTENTS

THE MYTH OF THE ARYAN INVASION OF INDIA

1. The Post-Colonial World

Our view of human history colors the perception of who we are in a fundamental way. It creates the infrastructure of ideas according to which we interpret the world. Like the limitations of our senses we seldom question the limitations of our historical view, which we take as a given fact, even though it changes with every generation. Each society creates an idea of history through which it interprets civilization in its own image. In the modern age science, technology and rational materialism have created an historical view that makes ancient Greece, in which the seeds of modern culture arose, the basis of civilization as a whole. It looks to the precursors of civilization in the ancient Near East, Sumeria and Egypt, from which the Greeks derived the rudiments of their culture. This view ignores or denigrates other ancient traditions like those of India, China or Mesoamerica as of little importance. Indeed if we examine books on world history today we discover that they are largely histories of modern Europe, with non-European cultures turned into a mere footnote, or simply dismissed as primitive, that is, not technologically advanced, however spiritually or artistically evolved they may have been.

In the post-colonial era, however, we are now questioning this Eurocentric and materialistic view of humanity. We are recognizing the value of traditional cultures and indigenous peoples, whose mistreatment and devaluation now appears on par with the destruction of our natural environment that we have been hastily promoting in the name of material progress. With a new understanding of depth psychology, mythology and comparative religion we are gaining a greater appreciation of spiritual ways of life, like the science of yoga, which developed outside of both the European and Middle Eastern cultural matrixes.

A number of racial, ethnic and religious groups have challenged their negative portrayal in modern Eurocentric historical accounts. For example, the European conquest of America, which was previously regarded as the benign expansion of advanced European civilization, is now being reinterpreted as a genocide of native peoples and destruction of their ancient cultures. Non-European cultures are no longer accepting the European interpretation of their histories, which not surprisingly makes their cultures inferior to that of Europe. This movement of historical rectification is bringing about a revolution in our view of history that is only just beginning and is bound to change our idea of who we are as human beings.

India is another country whose history has been greatly distorted by a colonial and materialistic European bias. India was the foremost of the British colonies and the center for the spiritual view of humanity that the materialistic mind has ever opposed. Now historians of ancient India are raising questions about the Eurocentric interpretation of Indian history and bringing forth new views that give greater validity to the traditional culture and literature of India which has always emphasized the spiritual life.

In this article we will examine important new discoveries in regard to ancient India that show the need for a radical reexamination of the history of the region. A careful study of the data today reveals that existing accounts of ancient India and thereby world history as well — particularly the Aryan invasion theory which is the cornerstone of the Eurocentric interpretation of India — *are contrary to all the evidence and need to be totally altered.* This is indeed a bold statement but, if true as the facts outlined below will indicate, requires changing the entire way in which Indian civilization has been evaluated.

2. The Aryan Invasion Theory

The main idea used to interpret the ancient history of India, which we still find in history books today, is the theory of the Aryan invasion. According to this account, which I will briefly summarize, India was invaded and conquered by nomadic light-skinned Indo-European tribes (Aryans) from Central Asia around 1500-1000 BC. They overran an earlier and more advanced dark-skinned Dravidian civilization from which they took most of what later became Indian civilization. In the process they never gave the indigenous people, from whom they took their civilization, the proper credit but eradicated all evidence of their conquest. All that the Aryans really added of their own was their language (Sanskrit, of an Indo-European type) and their priestly cult of caste that was to become the bane of later Indic society.

The so-called Aryans, the original people behind the Vedas, the oldest scriptures of Hinduism, were reinterpreted by this modern theory not as sages and seers — the rishis and yogis of Hindu historical tradition — but as primitive plunderers. Naturally this cast a shadow on the Hindu religion and culture as a whole.

The so-called pre-Aryan or Dravidian civilization is said to be indicated by the large urban ruins of what has been called the "Indus Valley culture" (as most of its initial sites were on the Indus river), or "Harappa and Mohenjodaro," after its two initially largest sites. In this article we will call this civilization the "Harappan" as its sites extend far beyond the Indus river. It is now dated from 3100 to 1900 BC. By the invasion theory Indic civilization is proposed to have been the invention of a pre-Vedic civilization and the Vedas, however massive their literature, are merely the products of a dark age following its destruction. Only the resurgence of the pre-Vedic culture in post-Vedic times is given credit for the redevelopment of urban civilization in India.

The Aryan invasion theory has become the basis of the view that Indian history has primarily been one of invasions from the West, with little indigenous coming from India itself either in terms of populations or cultural innovations. The history of India appears as a series of outside invasions: Aryans, Persians, Greeks, Scythians, Huns, Arabs, Turks, Portuguese, British, and so on. Following this logic, it has even led to the idea that the Dravidians also originally were outsiders. The same logic has resulted in the proposition of a Dravidian migration into India from Central Asia, a few thousand years before the Aryan invasion, overrunning the original aboriginal people of the region (now thought to be represented by the tribals of the area). Though "Dravidian invasion" has not been brought into the same prominence as the Aryan invasion theory, it shows the same bias that for civilization we must look to Western peoples and cultures and not to India as any separate center of civilization.

The Aryan invasion theory is not a mere academic matter, of concern only to historians. In the colonial era the British used it to divide India along north-south, Aryan-Dravidian lines — an interpretation various south Indian politicians have taken up as the cornerstone for their political projection of Dravidian identity. The Aryan invasion theory is the basis of the Marxist critique of Indian history where caste struggle takes the place of class struggle with the so-called pre-Aryan indigenous peoples turned into the oppressed masses and the invading Aryans turned into the oppressors, the corrupt ruling elite. Christian and Islamic missionaries have used the theory to denigrate the Hindu religion as a product of barbaric invaders, and promote their efforts to convert Hindus. Every sort of foreign ideology has employed it to try to deny India any real indigenous civilization so that the idea of the rule of foreign governments or ideas becomes acceptable. Even today it is not uncommon to see this theory appearing in Indian newspapers to uphold modern, generally Marxist or anti-Hindu political views. From it comes the idea that there is really no cohesive Indian identity or Hindu religion but merely a collection of the various peoples and cultures who have come to the subcontinent, generally from the outside. Therefore a re-examination of this issue is perhaps the most vital intellectual concern for India today.

The Aryan invasion theory was similarly applied to Europe and the Middle East. It proposed that the Indo-Europeans were invaders into these regions as well in the second millennium BC. Thereby it became the basis for maintaining a Near Eastern view of civilization, which places the earliest civilization in Mesopotamia and tries to derive all others from it. Thereby the invasion theory has been used to try to subordinate Eastern religions, like Hinduism and Buddhism, to Western religions like Christianity and Islam, which are supposed to represent the original civilization of the world from Adam, the Biblical original man, who came from Mesopotamia. This is the case even though the ancient civilization which has been found in Mesopotamia resembles far more the Hindu, with its Gods and Goddesses and temple worship, than it does these later aniconic traditions.

The Aryans invasion theory has been used for political and religious advantage in a way that is perhaps unparalleled for any historical idea. Changing it will thereby alter the very fabric of how we interpret ourselves and our civilization East and West. It is bound to meet with resistance, not merely on rational grounds but to protect the ideologies which have used it to their benefit. Even when evidence to the contrary is presented, it is unlikely that it will be given up easily. The evidence which has come up and disproved it, has led to the reformulation of the theory along different lines, altering the aspects of it that have become questionable but not giving up its core ideas.

Yet with the weight of much new evidence today, *the Aryan invasion theory no longer has any basis to stand on, however it is formulated.* There is no real evidence for any Aryan invasion — whether archaeological, literary or linguistic — and no scholar working in the field, even those who still accept some outside origin for the Vedic people (the so-called Aryans), accepts the theory in its classical form of the violent invasion and destruction of the Harappan cities by the incoming Aryans.

Four main points have emerged, which this article will elaborate:

1. The main center of Harappan civilization is the newly rediscovered Sarasvati river of Vedic fame. While the Indus river has about *three dozen* important Harappan sites, the Sarasvati has over *five hundred.* The drying up of the

Sarasvati brought about the end of the Harappan civilization around 1900 BC. As the Vedas know of this river they cannot be later than the terminal point for the river or different than the Harappans who flourished on its banks. The Harappan culture should be renamed "the Sarasvati culture." The Vedic culture must have been in India long before 2000 BC.

2. No evidence of any significant invading populations have been found in ancient India, nor have any destroyed cities or massacred peoples been unearthed. The so-called massacre of Mohenjodaro that Wheeler, an early excavator of the site claimed to find, has been found to be only a case of imagination gone wild. The sites were abandoned along with the ecological changes that resulted in the drying up of the Sarasvati.

3. The so-called Aryan cultural traits like horses, iron, cattle-rearing or fire worship have been found to be either indigenous developments (like iron) or to have existed in Harappan and pre-Harappan sites (like horses and fire worship). No special Aryan culture in ancient India can be differentiated apart from the indigenous culture.

4. A more critical reading of Vedic texts reveals that Harappan civilization, the largest of the ancient world, finds itself reflected in Vedic literature, the largest literature of the ancient world.[1] Vedic literature was previously not related to any significant civilization but merely to "the destruction of Harappa." How the largest literature of the ancient world was produced by illiterate nomadic peoples as they destroyed one of the great civilizations of the ancient world, is one of the absurdities that the Aryan invasion leads to, particularly when the urban literate Harappans are not given any literature of their own remaining.

---

[1] Navaratna Rajaram and David Frawley, *Vedic Aryans and the Origins of Civilization: A Literary and Scientific Perspective* (Ottawa and New Delhi, World Heritage Press, 1994).

Putting these points together we now see that the Vedas show the same development of culture, agriculture and arts and crafts as Harappan and pre-Harappan culture. Vedic culture is located in the same region as the Harappan, north India centered on the Sarasvati river. The abandonment of the invasion theory solves the literary riddle. Putting together Vedic literature, the largest of the ancient world, with the Harappan civilization, the largest of the ancient world, a picture emerges of ancient India as the largest civilization of the ancient world with the largest and best preserved literature — a far more logical view, and one that shows India as a consistent center from which civilization has spread over the last five thousand years.

Therefore it is necessary to set aside the discredited idea of the Aryan invasion and rewrite the textbooks in light of the new model, which is an organic and indigenous development of civilization in India from 6500 BC with no break in continuity or evidence of significant intrusive populations such as the invasion theory requires.[2] Ancient India now appears not as a broken civilization deriving its impetus from outside invaders but as the most continuous and consistent indigenous development of civilization in the ancient world, whose literary record, the ancient Vedas, remains with us today.

Based on such new evidence an entire group of scholars has arisen from both India and the West who reject the Aryan invasion theory on various grounds considering the evidence of archeology, skeletal remains, geography, mathematics, astronomy, linguistics and so on. Such individuals include S.R. Rao, Navaratna Rajaram, Subhash Kak, James Schaffer, Mark Kenoyer, S.P. Gupta, Bhagwan Singh, B.G. Siddharth, K.D. Sethna, K.D. Abhyankar, P.V. Pathak, Shrikant Talageri, S. Kalyanaraman, B.B. Chakravorty, George Feuerstein, and my-

---

[2] For the archaeological work in this regard note *Chronologies in Old World Archeology*, Third Edition, edited by Robert W. Ehrich, Vol. 1 (University of Chicago Press, 1992), Chapter 26, 'The Indus Valley, Baluchistan, and Helmand Traditions: Neolithic through Bronze Age.'

self, to name a few.[3] Their views generally support those of earlier Indian scholars and yogis, like Sri Aurobindo or B.G. Tilak, who proposed a Vedic nature for the civilization of India going back to early ancient times.

The few scholars today who continue to hold an outside origin for the Aryans have also generally given up the invasion/ destruction idea, though they may still be proposing an outside origin for the Aryans. They are proposing an Aryan migration, diffusion, or mixing with indigenous people which is quite different from the violent and intrusive form of the original Aryan invasion idea (note Romila Thapar in this regard[4]). Some of these scholars accept an Aryan element in the Harappan culture itself, owing to Vedic traits like fire altars which have been found in Harappan sites, though they still may not regard the Harappan culture as a whole as Aryan.

Yet whether the Vedic people were the original people of India, which is the majority view, or whether they migrated gradually into India, *the image of the invading and destructive Aryans is totally discredited and should be removed.* The image of the Indo-Aryans as proto-fascists, which is how the Aryan invasion theory has been used to represent them, is totally false. The Idea misrepresents Hindu-Vedic culture, which has traditionally been peaceful and never invaded any country, inflames Dravidian sentiments, and casts a shadow of violence on ancient India for no real reason.

In this article I will summarize the main points which demonstrate the invalidity of the invasion theory. This is a complex subject which I have dealt with in depth in my book *Gods, Sages and Kings: Vedic Light on Ancient Civilization,*[5] for those interested in a more extensive examination.

---

[3] For several such views note B.U. Nayak and N.C. Ghosh, *New Trends in Indian Art and Archeology*, (New Delhi, Aditya Prakashan, 1992).

[4] Romila Thapar, "Archeology and Language at the Roots of Ancient India", *Journal of the Asiatic Society of Bombay,* Vol. 64-66, 1989-1991.

[5] Salt Lake city, USA, Passage Press, 1991 and New Delhi, India, Motilal Banarsidass, 1993.

3. Basis of the Aryan Invasion Theory

We should first note that the Aryan invasion theory was foreign to the history of India, whether north or south, *which has no literary or historical record of any such event.* Prior to the invention of the idea by nineteenth century European scholars there was no tradition of an Aryan invasion anywhere in India, in either contemporary or ancient records. The so-called conquering of a country as big as a subcontinent left no record either in the so-called conquering or so-called conquered people. It vanished without a memory from the whole of India.

If we examine Hindu literature we see that the Vedas show an expansion of civilization both east and west from their most sacred Sarasvati river which flowed west of Delhi, which was also the homeland of Harappan culture. The Purāṇas show an expansion from the Ganges, the site of later classical Indian culture. Even the Tamil kings, the so-called conquered Dravidians, proudly called themselves Aryans and traced their dynasties back to Vedic kings. Hindu literature north and south shows an expansion from points within India, not an entry into India from a point on the outside.

There has been an attempt by modern scholars to read the Aryan invasion into Vedic literature. Such so-called literary evidence for the invasion, which is continually adjusted relative to new archaeological data, generally consists of misreading Vedic texts, taking out a few lines that appear to support such ideas, and ignoring everything to the contrary. This literary side I will focus on most in this article because it reflects the main misconceptions created by the invasion theory, but let us examine the archeology as well.

The most interesting point is that the Aryan invasion idea was not originally based on any archaeological evidence at all, as in the nineteenth century when it was proposed very little excavation of India had been done. It was the product of linguistic speculation — that similarities between Indo-European languages require an original homeland for the Indo-Europeans somewhere in Europe or Central Asia — from which migrations and invasions occurred, which eventually reached India.

Yet even accepting such a linguistic necessity (which is not beyond question), an invasion or migration (which are quite different phenomena) could have been in 6000 BC as well as 1500 BC. In fact an earlier date is more likely, given the complexity of Indo-European cultures and their existence from India to Europe, an extensive region of the globe, by 1500 BC. It would have taken some time for these cultures to have formed and moved, particularly in early ancient times when cultural developments were much slower than today.

The movement of the Aryans could have as well been from India to the west rather than from the west into India, as subtropical India with its vast river systems is more able to produce the necessary populations for such migrations than barren Central Asia or cold eastern Europe, which even today are very difficult to inhabit. Such movements certainly do not require the violent type of invasion that the Aryan invasion portrays and the image of the Vedic Aryans as plunderers.

To build up the entire history of a country as big as a subcontinent upon a new linguistic approach which had never proved itself as a valid tool of historical interpretation was indeed hasty, and not surprisingly has turned out to be erroneous. *Such linguistic "evidence" we should note is only speculation.* Linguistic evidence — which is an attempt to reconstruct a proto or original language from existent language fragments, locates cultures on the basis of certain words that exist in different languages and dates history by supposed rates of language change, and so on — is all soft evidence. In most cases the ancient form of languages has not survived, or exists only partially. It is only because the Vedas have been so well preserved that any such speculation could even be attempted. That we moderns coming from a totally different culture and world view can with a few language fragments reconstruct earlier ancient languages and the history of the cultures involved from them is indeed a great assumption!

Without verification by other sources linguistic arguments cannot carry any weight at all. Not surprisingly various linguists have proposed that linguistic evidence proves an original home for the Aryans everywhere from western China to Hungary, Scandinavia and Anatolia (modern Turkey), even India, in short everywhere we have found such peoples in historical times! Such linguistic speculation should not be used to override more solid literary and archaeological evidence. Now it can be shown that the Vedic literary evidence and ancient Indian archaeological evidence are in agreement, making such linguistic "evidence" to the contrary invalid.

To date there is no culture in ancient India that can be identified as that of the invading Aryans. There are no specific ruins, no burial sites, no agricultural practices, no pottery styles, in fact no artifacts of any kind that can be clearly attributed to the invading Aryans. There is no trail that they have left that can be traced back to any Central Asian homeland. Whatever of this nature has been proposed has not stood the test of time. There is nothing to separate the so-called Aryans from the non-Aryans in terms of culture, religion or populations.

Recent finds in archeology have filled in the gap of time from the Harappan to the post-Harappan age (1900-1000 BC), which was originally regarded as the "Vedic dark age" wherein the Aryan invasion could be placed because there was no evidence of anything to the contrary. What was thought to be a post-Harappan decline owing to the invading Aryans has now been found not to have merely a relocation and development of Harappan culture following the drying up of the Sarasvati along less urban lines but preserving all the main elements of Harappan culture, including an expansion of the number of villages. While there were fewer cities in the post-Harappan age, Dr. S.R. Rao has found two sites — Dwaraka and Bet Dwaraka in Gujarat —which were large urban sites. Dwaraka, dated around 1500 BC, was in fact larger than Mohenjodaro, the largest Harappan site.[6]

In one of his most recent papers on the subject archeologist Jim G. Schaffer of Case Western Reserve University in Cleveland, Ohio, U.S.A. states in bold:

> **The shift by Harappan groups, and perhaps, other Indus Valley cultural mosaic groups, is the only archaeologically documented west-to-east movement of human populations in South Asia before the first half of the first millennium BC.[7]**

The Aryan invasion theory requires a west-to-east movement of populations from Central Asia into India, evidence for which in ancient India does not exist. The relocation of populations within India that Schaffer speaks of is from the Sarasvati region, when it dried up, to the Ganges region, in which the continuity of culture was preserved. This agrees with the Hindu literary record which places the Vedic civilization on the Sarasvati, shifting to the Puranic civilization on the Ganges. *The only real west-to-east movement in ancient India was of the Harappan (Sarasvati) peoples themselves, not of any outside invaders.*

Let us continue and examine the details of the invasion theory and how they have been invalidated.

4. Aryan as Race or Language

The Aryan invasion theory is based upon the idea that Aryan represents a particular group of people. In the classical view of the Aryan invasion the Aryans are a particular ethnic group, speaking a particular language. However, in Vedic literature Aryan is not the name of the Vedic people and their descendants. It is a title of honor and respect given to certain groups for good

---

    [6] S.R. Rao, *Dawn and Devolution of the Indus Civilization* (New Delhi, Aditya Prakashan, 1991).

    [7] Jim G. Schaffer and Diane A. Lichtenstein, "The Cultural Tradition and Paleoethnicity in South Asian Archeology", to appear in *Language, Material Culture and Ethnicity: The Indo-Aryans in Ancient South Asia* (Berlin, Mouton, DeGruyter).

or noble behavior. In this regard even the Buddha calls his teaching Aryan, Arya Dharma; the Jains also call themselves Aryans, as did the ancient Persians. For this reason one should call the Vedic people simply the "Vedic people" and not the Aryans. If one takes Aryan in the Vedic sense, it would not be like talking of the invasion of good people, as if goodness were a racial or linguistic quality!

The Aryan invasion theory proposed that the Aryans belonged to a particular racial stock — generally the blond and blue-eyed Nordic Caucasians or at least fair-skinned European types (for which no real evidence in ancient India exists either) — and spoke only one language, Vedic Sanskrit (though this appears from the beginning as a priestly language, not a common dialect). The Aryans were said to have looked down upon those of different racial features or those who spoke different (presumably non-Indo-European) languages. The invasion theory thereby projected various cultural biases — that Vedic culture was racist or that it was based upon some sort of linguistic chauvinism. In short it cast an aspersion of prejudice and intolerance upon a culture before there had been any real examination of it. Meanwhile all the changes in ancient India were defined by this conflict of racial or linguistic groups, and all other factors of social change were ignored.

The idea of a monolithic cultural group chauvinistically promoting ethnic and linguistic purity is the product of nineteenth century colonial thinking. It mirrors nineteenth century European racial views of Humanity, in which dark-skinned people were regarded as inferior and used as slaves. It is quite different than the Hindu and Vedic view that the One Being masks itself in numerous names and forms which are all ultimately the same. Such a monolithic group is incompatible with the image of the Aryans as nomads, who as a scattered and disorganized group could not have had such a uniform idea of their own identity and been able to impose it upon a larger population of more civilized peoples.

The Aryan invasion theory is an example of European colonialism turned into an historical model. Its simplicity is compelling but also questionable. Race and language are not the only factors in the development of civilization. Religious or economic factors, which cut across racial and linguistic divisions, often overwhelm them. For example, ancient Mesopotamia had a number of ethnic groups, people of different language families, a composite of many religions, and yet many common cultural elements can be found through the Sumerian, Babylonian and Assyrian civilizations of the region.

This monolithic race/language approach to history appears to be overly simplistic, particularly in the twentieth century wherein the pluralism of culture (a common Hindu idea) is becoming recognized. The history of a big country like India is likely to be much more complex than such facile stereotypes.

Migration theories were in vogue in nineteenth and early twentieth century thought, which had witnessed the great migrations from Europe to America. Any new cultural innovation discovered in archeology was made the product of a new migration. A new pottery style found in a culture was attributed to a new people coming into the area. However migration is usually not the main factor in social change, which usually occurs owing to internal factors. Otherwise we would have to explain the invasion or migration of the computer people to explain current changes in civilization! Now archaeologists are moving away from such migration theories and looking more for the internal factors that could cause such changes. If such internal factors can be found — such as is the case in ancient India which shows an internal continuity of cultural developments going back to the pre-historic era — a migration is not necessary.

We should note that Vedic literature, with its many Gods and Goddesses who can be identified freely with one another (what Max Muller called henotheism), is clearly the product of a pluralistic culture and world view, not that of a monolithic culture (which Hinduism has never produced in the historical period either). Unity-in-multiplicity is the basic theme of the Vedas which state, "That which is the One Truth the seers speak in many ways (Rig Veda I.64)." This is not the philosophy of militant nomads but of a mature cultural complex in which many different cultural elements have been interwoven. Simplistic invasion/migration theories reducing cultural developments to movements of narrowly defined groups of people appear now to be out of date, and certainly do not mirror the Vedic view of the universe.

5. The Development of the Aryan Invasion Idea

European scholars following Max Muller in the nineteenth century decided that the Vedic people — whom they called the Aryans after a misinterpretation of that Vedic term — invaded India around 1500 BC. They were said to have overthrown the primitive and aboriginal culture of the time, which was thought to be Dravidian in nature, and brought a more advanced civilization to the land (though they themselves were still regarded as barbarians). The indigenous aborigines were identified as the Dasyus or inimical people mentioned in the Vedas.

The rationale behind the late date for the Vedic culture given by Max Muller was totally speculative and based only on linguistic grounds. He had assumed that the five layers of the four Vedas and the Upanishads were each composed in two hundred year periods before the Buddha at 500 BC, as they were in existence by that time.

However, the rates of change for languages are quite speculative, particularly for those languages, like Sanskrit or Latin, which became scriptural or scholarly languages apart from common dialects. There are more changes of language within Vedic Sanskrit itself than there are in classical Sanskrit since Panini, regarded as a figure of around 500 BC, or a period of 2500 years. As classical Sanskrit has remained the same for that time period, the two hundred year strata for the Vedic language carries no weight at all. Each of these periods could have existed for any number of centuries, and the two hundred year figure is likely to be too short a figure.

The idea that the Aryans were a particular race was not accepted by everyone. Max Muller himself rejected it. Yet it has become ingrained in the Aryan theory so much that the common mind has accepted it as a fact. This idea of the Aryans as a particular race, speaking a particular language, I call the "first birth" of the Aryan invasion theory. Yet in its first form the Aryan invasion was of people who were as or more advanced in culture than the indigenous aborigines that they overcame.

Harappa and Mohenjodaro were not excavated until the early part of the twentieth century. *As by this time the 1500 BC date for the Vedic people was accepted and since Harappa dated before this it was uncritically accepted that the Harappan culture must be pre-Vedic.* The Aryan invasion theory was rewritten to make the Aryans the uncivilized destroyers of the civilized Dravidian-Harappan culture. Yet few questioned this rewriting of the Aryan invasion theory in light of new evidence. This we could call the "second birth" of the Aryan invasion theory — in which the Vedic Aryans were not only violent and intolerant but the destroyers of one of the great civilizations of antiquity — which makes the Vedic Aryans appear as proto-Nazis. *This is the view of the Aryan invasion that is most commonly accepted today, even after it has been accepted by all scholars that there is no evidence of any Harappan cities being destroyed by invaders.* Because it is the most negative view of the Aryans, it has been most seized upon by the opposing Hindu or Vedic culture.

Meanwhile other archaeologists in the early part of this century pointed out that in the middle of the second millennium BC, various Indo-Europeans appear in the Middle East, wherein Indo-European Hittites, Mittani and Kassites conquered and ruled Mesopotamia for some centuries. A Greek invasion of Europe was also postulated for this period, as it marked the period when the Minoan culture declined, which was assumed to be non-Indo-European. Hence an Aryan invasion of Greece and the Middle East was proposed. An Aryan invasion of India was regarded as another version of this same migratory movement of Indo-European peoples around the middle of the second millennium BC, which became one of the most dramatic migrations in the history of the world and for which no real cause has ever been given.

On top of this, excavators of the Indus Valley culture, like Wheeler, thought that they had found evidence of destruction of the culture by an outside invasion, confirming the idea (though Wheeler's so-called skeletal evidence of the massacre of Mohenjodaro has long since been refuted it still appears in many historical accounts even today!)

Vedic culture was thus said to be that of primitive nomads who came out of Central Asia with their horse-drawn chariots and iron weapons, like the Indo-European Hittites in the Near East who were among the first to use iron weapons, and overthrew the cities of the more advanced Harappan culture, with their cruder culture yet superior battle tactics. It was pointed out that no horses, chariots or iron were discovered in Harappan sites, and since such things are mentioned in the Vedas, this culture must be pre-Vedic.

To support this theory other aspects of the Vedas were molded according to it. Vedic references to destruction of cities were related to Harappa. The Vedic metal *ayas* was said to be iron, though it is only a generic term meaning metal. Vedic references to the ocean were reduced to mean only the Indus river or some other large body of water in northwest India or Afghanistan. Vedic references to rivers from the Indus to the Ganges, which are merely a list of rivers, were interpreted to show a movement from the west to the east of India. The Aryan invasion theory was imposed on archaeological and literary evidence, even if it required altering the data.

This was how the Aryan invasion theory formed. The logic was inevitable. Once the image of invading Aryans was formed, it has to be drawn out to its ultimate form envisioning the Aryans like Atilla the Hun.

6. Mechanics of the Aryan Invasion

The Aryan invasion theory was invented to solve the riddle of languages. However, the invasion theory itself is filled with problems. We could say that the Aryan invasion theory is an attempt to solve one riddle by postulating another.

If such an invasion did occur, what could have caused it? Central Asia is not a very favorable region for producing populations even today, as we have already noted. How could it produce the populations necessary to overrun not only India but much of the Middle East and Europe? Ancient India was not uninhabited. After the long urban Harappan age it was highly populated at the time of the proposed invasion. Such populations could not have easily been overwhelmed, forced to move or be assimilated. After all it was not an organized conquest but a random movement of tribal peoples which is postulated for the Aryans.

What would cause the proto-Aryans to move, and in so many directions, to Europe, the Middle East and India? Generally when groups migrate it is in one direction. People do not abandon their homelands and move in all directions with such fury without a reason, particularly nomadic people who are wedded to their territory.

How could the primitive Aryans have been so successful in conquering the civilizations of the world from Greece to India, as well as imposing much of their culture, or at least language, on older and more sophisticated civilizations? Language, after all, is the most difficult aspect of culture to change. Many countries, for example, Europe under Christianity or Iran and Pakistan under Islam, have changed their religion but not their language. How could the primitive Aryans be so successful at doing this, when they were not only less sophisticated and less numerous than the peoples they overran but also illiterate?

We should note that Afghanistan is not an easy place to cross through even today. Even Alexander lost most of his army trying to cross this region by land. How could sufficient numbers of people have done it in ancient times so as to overwhelm the existent population of north India? In the historical period armies from Central Asia have been able to conquer north India at times. But they have not been able to change the population or to impose their language on the country. How could disorganized nomads, such as the Vedic people were supposed to have been, accomplish this and also remove any record or memory of what they had done?

To assume that the proto-Aryans were just simply vicious and had to ruthlessly conquer everyone, and that with some advantages like the use of the horse they were able to do so, does not work either. Such vicious conquests cause tremendous resistance in the conquered people which is not in evidence in ancient India, Greece or elsewhere where the Aryans have been found. The ancient Indo-European peoples did not have a reputation as being particularly cruel. In the ancient Middle East of the second and first millennium BC, for example — in which a number of Indo-European peoples existed like the Hittites, the Mittani and the Kassites — the reputation for cruelty did not go to them but to the Semitic Assyrians against whom they fought. While the Assyrians and Babylonians enslaved the Jews, it was the Persians, who called themselves Aryans, who released them from their captivity! In any case, no evidence of such movement of populations into India or destroyed cities has been found.

7. Harappan Civilization

After the formulation of the Aryan invasion theory, archeology did not stop. New finds continued. These however have gradually undermined the invasion theory.

Harappan civilization (3100-1900 BC) was the largest in the world up to its time. Harappan sites have now been found as far west as the coast of modern Iran, as far north as Turkestan on the Amu Darya (a region usually identified with the Aryans), as far northeast as the Ganges, and south to the Godavari river. A site has even been found on the coast of Arabia. Thousands of sites have been found with several cities, like Ganweriwala on the Sarasvati river and Dholavira near the ocean in Kutch, as large as the first two major cities found earlier, Harappa and Mohenjodaro. Most sites remain unexcavated and new explorations are likely to push the boundaries of this civilization yet further. A civilization of this size could not have been quickly or easily overrun by either migration or invasion.

Harappan culture maintained a continuity and uniformity that is unparalleled in cultures up to that date. The cities were the best planned of the era, with wide streets and excellent sewage systems. There was a uniformity of arts, crafts, weights and measures throughout the region. Such an organized civilization could not have so easily been taken over, nor could its cultural traditions, particularly its language, be very easily changed, much less eradicated.

It was originally proposed that the Harappan culture was ended abruptly by the Aryan invaders. Evidence however revealed that the sites were abandoned rather than destroyed, along with major ecological changes in the region, with shifting rivers, floods, and desertification of parts of the region, along with the drying up of the Sarasvati river which we have already noted. Unfortunately most historians, particularly from the West, did not know of the importance of the Sarasvati in Vedic literature and merely treated it as a river forgotten by everyone.

Because of this evidence some scholars have given up the idea that the Vedic people destroyed the Harappan culture, and proposed that the Vedic people came after the decline of the culture and merely took over the remnants of it. In this view it was the abandoned Harappan cities that the Aryans came to. But this view still usually portrayed the advent of the Aryans as violent. This post-Harappan violent invasion I would call "the third birth of the Aryan invasion theory," though it is unclear what they destroyed. It shows the theory already in question.

Other scholars proposed that the Aryans came into the Indus civilization itself during its later period and that Harappan culture was a composite of Aryan and non-Aryan elements, though there is nothing particularly composite about Harappan culture. Most scholars of such views would still like to portray the Aryan advent as violent though no proof for that has ever been found. Meanwhile no evidence of such migrations during the Harappan period has been found either.

8. Migration Rather than Invasion

Coming to the present time, given the facts that there was no destruction of Harappan cities and no evidence of any large scale migrations of people, the latest form of "the Aryans coming from the outside" (as for example, represented by Romila Thapar, who is a well-known Marxist historian generally opposed to Vedic culture) is of a gradual migration of small groups of pastoral peoples during the same period of the second millennium BC.

> It is now generally agreed that the decline of Harappan urbanism was due to environmental changes of various kinds, to political pressures and possible break in trading activities, and not to any invasion. Nor does the archaeological evidence register the likelihood of a massive migration from Iran into north-western India on such a scale as to overwhelm the existing cultures.
>
> If invasion is discarded then the mechanisms of migrations and occasional contacts come into sharper focus. The migrations appear to have been of pastoral cattle-herders who are prominent in the Avesta and the Rig Veda.[8]

From the ferocious Aryan hordes we have come down to mild pastoral migrants coming not with iron and chariots but only herds of cattle. This Aryan migration theory I call the "fourth birth of the Aryan invasion theory."

How small groups of pastoral migrants can accomplish

---

[8] Romila Thapar, "Archeology and Language at the Roots of Ancient India", *Journal of the Asiatic Society of Bombay*, Vol. 64-66, 1989-1991, pp. 259-260.

changing the language of a country as big as a subcontinent — which already had given birth to its own great civilization — and imposing their own culture and social system upon it, is highly improbable and almost absurd. An existent complex cultural order — such as ancient India indicates — can easily assimilate a few cattle herders moving in, but such groups cannot be given the credit to assimilate the whole culture of a big country. Cattle-herders only expand their territory gradually, and are not hard for existent populations to resist. Nor were the Harappans without their own cattle. They had a long tradition of cattle-rearing and could hardly be overwhelmed by an outside entrance of new cattle-breeders, particularly of a more primitive nature.

The Aryan migration explanation is even weaker than the invasion theory. *If such a migration was small and did not have any great impact on existing populations or leave any archaeo-logical record, as is the case, it could not have changed the region on the level of language either, which to reiterate is the hardest and slowest part of culture to change.* If the culture and population of a region did not change, it is ridiculous to think that the language changed independently of these. The migration theory is merely the invasion theory on its death bed, but even it is a great improvement over the usual Aryans-smashing-Harappa scenario which has captured the imagination of so many people.

The propositions of time, place and people for the Aryan invasion has continually shifted as it has always been a theory in search of facts, not one based on anything solid. The only logical conclusion of the continual retreat of the Aryan invasion theory from a destructive invasion to a pastoral migration is the complete abandonment of it. The continual changes in the theory relative to the data which disproves it only shows the invalidity at its core. The Aryan invasion has gone from a bang to whimper and will soon fade out altogether.

Many things thought to have been Vedic and not Harappan, are now found to have existed in the Harappan culture. To pre-

serve the Aryan invasion in the face of this evidence there are
even a few scholars who would give credit to the pre-Aryans for
most of what has been regarded as Vedic culture (like Shendge[9]),
including the Vedic Gods, the Brahmanical ritual, and most of
the Vedic hymns, as well as all the Puranas — which are all
claimed to have been stolen from the indigenous people and
retranslated — even the caste system itself has been said to be
pre-Aryan! In this instance the pre-Vedic people practised the
same rituals, chanted the same hymns as the Vedas, and were
ruled by their own priestly class, except in a non-Indo-European
language. This leads us to another absurdity. How could the
Vedic people translate the entire pre-Vedic culture into their own
massive and etymologically consistent corpus of literature and
ritual when they themselves are said to have been illiterate, while
the group whose culture they assumed in total could not preserve
any literary record of their own?

For such scholars even the Vedas themselves are the invention of pre-Vedic people! While this radical fringe may not be
taken seriously by other proponents of the invasion, such thinkers do have their point. Almost everything thought to be
Harappan can be found in the Vedas. If there was an Aryan
invasion it would have had to have taken over the existent culture in its entirely to account for this. Yet a more logical conclusion is that there was no invasion and Vedic and Harappan culture were never really different. Such absurdities are unneces-
sary when we accept that the Vedic people were present in India
from an early period and represent the civilization of India going
back to the pre-Harappan era.

Another recent view, which is also on the radical fringe that
other invasion proponents may not accept either, is that of Asko
Parpola.[10] He claims that the struggles mentioned in the Vedas

[9] Malati Shengde, *The Civilized Demons: The Harappans in Rig Veda,* New
Delhi, Abhinav Publications, 1977.

[10] Asko Parpola, *The Sky-Garment, A Study of the Harappan Religion and its
Relation to the Mesopotamian and later Indian Religions,* Helsinki, Finland:
Studia Orientalia 57, 1985.

were not in India at all, but in Afghanistan between two different groups of Indo-Iranian peoples. Even if we accept this view, which contradicts all the others, it totally fails to explain how the Vedic culture ever came to India, which is left a total blank. If the Vedas show the conquest of an early Indo-Iranian culture in Afghanistan, what is it that which shows the conquest of India? Certainly the Puranas do not. Moreover Parpola's view is refuted by the many references to places and rivers in India, like Sarasvati, Indus and Yamuna, which are common in the Rig Veda. Yet his view is also based upon a valid point. The conflicts represented in the Vedas are between people of the same basic cultural group or inter-Aryan battles, including the Iranians. As Parpola has assumed the invasion theory to be true, the only place for such an inter-Aryan conflict is Afghanistan, not in non-Aryan India. However, if we give up the invasion theory there is no need for such far fetched views.

9. The Rediscovery of the Sarasvati River

The retreat of the Aryan invasion theory has been accompanied by the rediscovery of the Sarasvati river of Vedic fame, though many scholars are still unaware of the connection of the river with the Vedas. Recent excavation has shown that the great majority of Harappan settlements were east, not west of Indus. The largest concentration of sites appears in an area of Punjab and Rajasthan along the dry banks of the Sarasvati (now called the Ghaggar) in the Thar desert. Hundreds of sites dot this river, which appears to have been the breadbasket of the culture. Mohenjodaro and Harappa, the first large Indus sites found, appear to be peripheral cities, mere gateways to the central Sarasvati region. The main sites are found in a region of northwestern India, which owing to the lack of water was never again a region of significant habitation. Hence it appears quite clearly that the sites were left owing to a shifting of the rivers and a drying out of the region which is a cause quite different than any invasion. The hand of Mother Nature is shown behind the population shift, not hostile invaders.

What is most interesting in this regard is that Vedic culture is traditionally said to have been founded by the sage Manu between the banks of the Sarasvati and Drishadvati rivers.[11] The Sarasvati is lauded as the main river in the Rig Veda and is the most frequently mentioned river in the text. It is said to be a great flood and to be wide, even endless in size, the greatest and most central river of the region of the seven rivers.[12] Sarasvati is said to be "pure in her course from the mountains to the sea."[13] The Vedic people were well acquainted with this river along its entire course and regarded it as their immemorial homeland.

The Sarasvati, as modern land studies now reveals, was indeed one of the largest rivers in India in ancient times (before 1900 BC) and was perhaps the largest river in India (before 3000 BC). In early ancient and pre-historic times, it drained the Sutlej and Yamuna, whose courses were much different than they are today.[14] However, the Sarasvati river went dry by the end of the Harappan culture and well before the so-called Aryan invasion or before 1500 BC.

How could the Vedic Aryans know of this river and establish their culture on its banks if it dried up some centuries before they arrived? Indeed the Sarasvati as described in the Rig Veda as a green and fertile region appears to more accurately show the river as it was prior to the Harappan culture as in the Harappan era it was already in decline. In the Brahmanas and Mahabharata the Sarasvati is said to flow in a desert and in the latter does not even reach the sea. The Sarasvati as a river is later replaced by

---

[11] Manu Samhita II.17-18.

[12] Note Rig Veda II.41.16; VI.61.8-13; I.3.12.

[13] Rig Veda VII.95.2. This is in a hymn of the rishi Vasishtha who has the greatest number of hymns in the Rig Veda.

[14] Studies from the Post-Graduate Research Institute of Deccan College, Pune, and the Central Arid Zone Research Institute (CAZRI), Jodhpur. Confirmed by use of MSS (multi-spectoral scanner) and Landsat satellite photography. Note MLBD Newsletter (Delhi, India: Motilal Banarsidass), November, 1989. Note also Sriram Sathe, *Bharatiya Historiography*, Hyderabad, India: Bharatiya Itihasa Sankalana Samiti, 1989, pp. 11-13.

the Ganges and is almost forgotten in Puranic literature. The stages of the drying up of the river can be traced in Vedic literature showing that the Vedic people did not merely come at the last phase of the river's life.

The existence of the Sarasvati as a great river was unknown until recent land studies. The very fact that the Vedic Sarasvati was traditionally only identified with a minor desert stream was previously regarded as proof of the invasion theory under the surmise that as the original Vedic river had no real counterpart in India, its real location must have been in another country like Afghanistan. Now that the great Indian Sarasvati has been found that evidence has been countered. If rivers in Afghanistan have Vedic names it is more likely an overflow of populations out of India, not the other way around, as no Afghani river has the size, location, or reaches the sea as did the Vedic Sarasvati. We have already noted Harappan sites in Afghanistan that would explain the naming of rivers there from larger Indian counterparts.

Therefore I am also proposing, along with many other scholars today both in India and the West, that the Harappan or Indus Valley civilization, should be renamed the "Sarasvati civilization," or at least "Indus-Sarasvati civilization." This would put an end to the misunderstanding of it, as the Sarasvati is the main river of the Vedas. The Indus and Sarasvati regions to the sea, which were the center of Harappan culture, are also the same geographical region of Vedic culture, which proves their identity.

10. The Vedic Image of the Ocean

The Rig Veda itself contains nearly a hundred references to ocean (*samudra*), as well as dozens of references to ships, and to rivers flowing into the sea. The main Vedic ancestor figures like Manu, Turvasha, Yadu and Bhujyu are flood figures, saved from across the sea. The Vedic God of the sea, Varuna, is the father of many Vedic seers like Vasishtha, the most famous of the seers, and the Bhrigu seers, the second most important seer family. Indeed the basic Vedic myth is of the God Indra who wins the seven rivers to flow into the sea? How could such a myth arise in the desert of Central Asia?[15]

To preserve the Aryan invasion idea it was assumed that the Vedic (and later Sanskrit) term for ocean, *samudra,* originally did not mean the ocean but any large body of water, especially the Indus river in the Punjab. Here the clear meaning of a term in the Rig Veda and later times — verified by rivers like Sarasvati mentioned by name as flowing into the sea — was altered to make the Aryan invasion theory fit. Yet if we look at the index to translation of the Rig Veda by Griffith for example, who held to this idea that *samudra* did not really mean the ocean, we find over seventy references to ocean or sea.[16] If *samudra* does not mean ocean why was it still translated as such? It is therefore without any basis to locate Vedic kings in Central Asia far from any ocean or from the massive Sarasvati river, which form the background of their land and the symbolism of their hymns.

Again the absence of archaeological data and the non-existence of any real Sarasvati river was used to justify this change of the meaning of terms. Now that the Sarasvati sites have been found as mentioned in the Veda, and ships and maritime trade in the Indus/Sarasvati culture, we should reexamine the Vedic references to *samudra* or ocean, and take them seriously.

As an interesting sidelight, it is now known that Aryan migrations to Sri Lanka from Gujarat began before 500 BC, if not much earlier, and Brahmi inscriptions have been found in Indonesia to about 300 BC, thus making the nomadic Aryans strangely and quickly turn into sea-faring traders and migrants. Yet such travel makes perfect sense if the Vedic people were

---

[15] David Frawley, *Gods, Sages and Kings: Vedic Secrets of Ancient Civilization*, Salt Lake City, Utah, USA: Passage Press, 1991 and Delhi, India: Motilal Banarsidass, 1993.

[16] R. Griffith, *The Hymns of the Rig Veda*, Delhi, India: Motilal Banarsidass, 1976.

familiar with the ocean at an early period. Meanwhile the Phoenicians were trading with the port of Ophir (Sopara, Surpāraka) north of Bombay during the time of King Solomon, circa. 975 BC. This also shows the Vedic people engaging in a maritime trade from central India at a period much too early for the Aryan invasion of 1500-1000 BC.

11. Horses, Chariots and Iron

All the main points of the Aryan invasion in its various incarnations have been disproved. The absence of horses, spoked wheels and iron in Harappan sites have been key points. Further excavations have discovered horses not only in Harappan but also in pre-Harappan sites, and in other sites in India from Karnataka to the Ganges region indicating an indigenous breed of horses in ancient India.

> The discovery of bones of Equus caballus Linn. (the true horse) from so many Harappan sites and that too right from the lowest levels clearly establishes that the true domesticated horse was very much in use.[17]

The use of the horse has been proven for the whole range of ancient Indian history. It was absurd to think that the Harappans did not have horses anyway, considering that Harappan sites included Afghanistan which definitely had horses and that Harappan trade with Central Asia would have included the horse anyway as it did the camel.

It is true that we do not find horses represented extensively in the iconography of ancient India, though there are Harappan horse figures, but iconography is not a representation of the actual fauna and flora of a country but only certain mythic images. That the unicorn is a common Harappan image, for example, does not prove that unicorns were a common animal

---

[17] A.K. Sharma, "The Harappan Horse Was Buried Under the Dunes", *Purātattva* 23.

during Harappan times. The horse is not common in later Indian iconography either, though we know the animal was commonly used.

Most interestingly the enemies of the Vedic people, the Dāsas or Dasyus, are also described in the Rig Veda as possessing a wealth in horses, which the Aryans win from them or receive as gifts from them. In fact one Dāsa Balbutha gives a Vedic seer a gift of 60,000 horses.[18] There is no battle between a horse and a non-horse culture in Vedic literature either. On the other hand, the famous Vedic Brahma bull is everywhere in ancient Indian iconography and throughout the Harappan culture, as are many other Vedic symbols like swastikas.

Evidence of the wheel, and an Indus seal showing a spoked wheel as used in chariots, has been found, suggesting the usage of chariots in at least the later Harappan period. The whole idea of nomads with chariots is itself questionable. Chariots are not the vehicles of nomads. Chariots are the vehicles of an urban elite or aristocracy, as in their usage in Rome, Greece and the ancient Middle East. Chariots are appropriate mainly in ancient urban cultures with much flat land, of which the broad river plain of north India was the most suitable. Chariots are unsuitable for crossing mountains and deserts, as the Aryan invasion requires. Meanwhile the term *"aśvārohī"* or one who mounts horses does not occur in the Rig Veda, showing no basis for the idea of the Vedic people as mounted horsemen from the steppes.

That the Vedic culture used iron — and must date later than the introduction of iron around 1500 BC — revolves around the meaning of the Vedic term *"ayas"*, interpreted according to the invasion theory as iron. *Ayas* in other Indo-European languages like Latin or German usually means copper, bronze or ore generally, not specifically iron. It is the basis of the English word ore and traced to the old Indo-European root "Ais, (a lump of)

---

[18] Rig Veda VIII. 46.22.32. Note also Rig Veda III.34.9.

bronze or copper, later used to designate iron."[19] There is no reason to insist that in such earlier Vedic times, *ayas* meant iron, particularly since other metals are not mentioned in the Rig Veda (except gold which is much more commonly referred to than *ayas*). Moreover, the Atharva and Yajur Vedas speak of different colors of metals along with *ayas* (such as red and black), with the black being the likely candidate for iron.[20] Hence it is clear that *ayas* generally meant metal and not specifically iron, most likely copper as in the Rig Veda it is compared to gold in its lustre and can be a synonym for gold.

Moreover, the inimical peoples in the Rig Veda, not only have horses, they use *ayas*, even for making their cities, as do the Vedic people themselves.[21] There is nothing in Vedic literature to show that either the Vedic culture was an iron-based culture or that their enemies were not. Both had the same metal whatever it was. The Vedic battle was between people of the same cultural complex including horses, *ayas* and chariots and does not reflect the cultural divide proposed by the Aryan invasion.

Early Vedic civilization, as evidenced in the Rig Veda, centers around the use of *ayas* or copper, barley (*yava*) as the main grain and cattle as the main domesticated animal. Pre-Harappan sites in India show copper, barley and cattle as the basis of the civilization. In Harappan times rice and wheat were also used, such as are mentioned in later Vedic texts like Atharva Veda. The general civilization shown in the Vedas reflects both Harappan and pre-Harappan eras and shows the development between them.

12. Destroyers of Cities

The Rig Veda describes its Gods as "destroyers or conquerors of cities." This was used to regard the Vedic as a primitive

---

[19] Eric Partridge, *A Short Etymological Dictionary of Modern English Origins*, New York: MacMillan, 1970, p. 457.
[20] For example Shukla Yajur Veda XVIII.13.
[21] For example, Rig Veda II.20.8; IV.27.1; VII.95.1.

nomadic culture that destroys cities and is opposed to urban civilization. However, there are many verses in the Rig Veda that speak of the Aryans as having cities of their own and being protected by cities up to a hundred in number. Aryan Gods like Indra, Agni, Sarasvati and the Adityas are praised like a city.[22] Many ancient kings, including those of Egypt and Mesopotamia, had titles like destroyer or conqueror of cities (which latter may be the real meaning of such terms, not reducing the cities to rubble but merely winning them). So does the great Hindu God Shiva who is called the destroyer of the three cities, *Tripurahara*. This does not turn them into nomads. Destruction of cities happens in modern wars; this does not make those who do this nomads either. Hence the idea of the Vedic culture as destroying but not building cities is based upon ignoring what the Vedas actually say. In fact the cities destroyed or conquered are often in the Rig Veda identified as those of other Vedic peoples, like the seven cities destroyed by Sudās whose enemies were mainly Vedic people (note section on Vedic peoples below).

However, since recent evidence shows that the Indus cities were abandoned and not destroyed, the idea of the Vedic Aryans as destroyers of cities has also vanished from the interpretations of those who still hold to an Aryan invasion or migration.

The Vedic struggle was between groups in the same cultural context who had horses, *ayas* (probably copper), barley and cities. It cannot refer to any battle between the invading Aryans and indigenous Harappans but appears to reflect indigenous conflicts of Harappan or pre-Harappan era, which must have existed in India then as in other ancient civilizations.

13. Vedic and Indus Religions

The interpretation of the religion of the Harappan culture — made incidentally by scholars such as Wheeler who were not religious scholars and had little knowledge of the Hindu religion

---

[22] Rig Veda VII.3.7; VII.15.14; VI.48.8; I.166.8; I.189.2; VII.95.1.

— was that its religion was different than the Vedic and more like the Shaivite religion in which Shiva is the supreme divinity. This was based on the examination of a handful of seals and symbols found in the ruins. Hence the Harappan religion was thought by them to be a kind of early Dravidian Shaivism. However, further excavations — both in Indus Valley sites in Gujarat, like Lothal, and those in Rajasthan, like Kalibangan — show large number of fire altars like those used in the Vedic religion, along with bones of oxen, potsherds, shell jewelry and other items used in the rituals described in the Vedic Brahmanas.[23] Vedic-like fire altars are more common in earlier than later Indus ruins. As fire altars are the most typical feature of Vedic culture, such finds associate the Vedic with Harappan culture from the beginning.

That the Harappan culture appeared non-Vedic to its excavators may be attributed to their lack of knowledge of Hindu culture generally, wherein Vedism and Shaivism are the same basic tradition. We must remember that ruins do not necessarily have one interpretation. Nor does the ability to discover ruins necessarily give the ability to interpret them correctly. Ancient India, like Egypt, had many deities and could not have been dominated by one only. It would have included Shiva, who as Rudra is already prominent in the Yajur and Atharva Vedas which appear to correspond with the Harappan age.

We also note that Shiva is the deity of the Ganges region which became the center of Indic civilization in the post-Harappan era. Vedic deities, like Indra and Agni, are those of the Sarasvati river to which the Harappan era belongs. Moreover Indra and Shiva have many common traits being the king of the Gods, the destroyer of cities, terrible or fierce in nature, the dancer, the lord of the Word, possessing a wife named power or Shakti, etc. There is no real divide between them.

Unfortunately certain Dravidian politicians and certain

---

[23] S.R. Rao, *Lothal and the Indus Civilization* (Bombay, India: Asia Publishing House, 1973), p.140; note also pp. 37 and 141.

Shaivite religious groups have uncritically accepted the Aryan invasion idea as it gives greater credence to their own traditions. In this regard they have only fallen into the trap of the invasion theory, which is to turn various Indic cultural elements against each other, rather than promote their commonality.

14. The So-called Racial War in the Vedas

The Vedic people were thought to have been a fair-skinned race like the Europeans owing to the Vedic idea of a war between light and darkness. To support this it was pointed out that the Vedic people were regarded as children of the light or children of the sun. However, this idea of a war between light and darkness exists in most ancient cultures both Indo-European and non-Indo-European, including the Egyptian and the Persian, whose ancient Zoroastrian religion is most dominated by this duality. It is also mirrored in the Biblical battle between God and Satan. Why don't we interpret these traditions as wars between light and dark-skinned people? It is a mythic metaphor, not a cultural statement. All the statements that refer to the inimical people in the Vedas as dark are simply part of this light-darkness analogy, the demons of the darkness versus the Sun God and his powers of light.

Moreover, no real traces of such a white race are found in ancient India.

Anthropologists have observed that the present population of Gujarat is composed of more or less the same ethnic groups as are noticed at Lothal in 2000 BC. Similarly, the present population of the Punjab is said to be ethnically the same as the population of Harappa and Rupar four thousand years ago. Linguistically the present day population of Gujarat and Punjab belongs to the Indo-Aryan language speaking group. The only inference that can be drawn from the anthropological and linguistic evidences adduced above is that the Harappan population in the Indus Valley and Gujarat in 2000 BC was composed of two or more groups, the more dominant among them having very close ethnic affinities with the present day Indo-Aryan speaking population of India.[24]

In other words *there is no racial evidence of an Indo-Aryan invasion of India, or of any populations that have been driven out of north India to the south, but only of a continuity of the same group of people who have traditionally considered themselves to be Aryan in culture.* There is no evidence of such a racial war archaeologically and the Vedic literary evidence appears only to be a twisting of metaphors. It would be like turning the Vedic prayer to lead us from darkness to light into a prayer to save us from dark-skinned people and ally us with those of white skin!

15. Vedic Peoples

Battles mentioned in the Rig Veda, whether between those called Aryans or Dasyus, are largely between the "five peoples" (*pancha mānava*). These five are identified as the Turvashas, Yadus, Purus, Anus and Druhyus, which the Puranas describe as originating from the five sons of Yayati, an early Vedic king in the lunar dynasty descended from Manu, and the son of Nahusha. These peoples, both Dasyus and Aryans, are also called Nahushas in the Rig Veda.[25] Of the five the main people of the Rig Veda are the Purus who are usually located on the Sarasvati river or the central region. The Yadus are placed in the south and west in Gujarat, Rajasthan and Maharashtra up to Mathura in the north. The Anus are placed in the north. The Druhyus are placed in the west and the Turvashas southeast. These are the directions given to them in the Puranas.[26]

In the original Puranic story there were two groups of

---

[24] Ibid., p.158
[25] Rig Veda VII.6.5; VII.95.2
[26] Vishnu Purana IV.10.16-8

people, the Devas and Asuras, or godly and ungodly people, who had various conflicts. Both had Brahmin gurus, the Angirasas for the Suras (Devas) and the Bhrigus for the Asuras. Both these Brahmin groups we might add were responsible for many teachings in ancient India, including the Upanishads. The battles between the Devas and Asuras involved a struggle between their gurus.

King Yayati, the father of the five Vedic peoples and a follower of the Angirasas, had two wives, Devayani, the daughter of Shukra of the Bhrigu seers, and Sharmishtha, the daughter of Vrishaparvan, king of the Asuras. Turvasha and Yadu were sons of Yayati by Devayani of the Bhrigus. Anu, Druhyu and Puru were sons of Yayati by Sharmishtha of the Asuras.[27] Yayati's story shows that the five Vedic people were born of an alliance of Aryan and Asuric kings, and their Angirasa and Bhrigu seers.

Vrishaparvan and Shukra appear to have come from southwest India, Gujarat, as the Bhrigus were descendants of Varuna, God of the sea, and have always been associated with this region of India (for example, their city Bhrigukaccha or modern Bharuch near Baroda). In the Puranic story their territory bordered on that of Yayati, who happened upon both Devayani and Sharmishtha, while hunting.

Hence three of the original five Vedic peoples had Asuric blood in them through their mother. Puru, whose group ultimately predominated, had Asuric blood, whereas the Yadus, who were most criticized in Vedic and Puranic literature, had no Asuric blood but rather that of the Brahmins. In this story we see that both groups of people — thought by the Aryan invasion theory to be the invading Aryans and the indigenous peoples — had the same religion and ancestry.

These five peoples were styled either Arya or Dasyu, which mean something like good or bad, holy or unholy according to their behavior. Their designation can shift quickly. The descen-

---

[27] Vishnu Purana IV.10

dants of an Aryan king can be called Dasyu or its equivalent (Rakshasa, Dasa, Asura etc.), if their behavior changes.

For example, in the most important battle in the Rig Veda, the famous battle of the Ten Kings (*Dāśarājna*), victorious Sudas, regarded as a Puru king, and located on the Sarasvati river, includes among his enemies called Dasyu groups of the five Vedic peoples like the Anus, Druhyus, Turvashas, and even Purus.[28] However, the sons of Sudas themselves fall and in Brahmanical and Puranic literature are themselves called Rakshasas or demons for killing the sons of the great rishi Vasishtha.[29] Meanwhile the Kavashas, a seer family, listed among the defeated enemies of Sudas[30] appear again in the Brahmanas and Upanishads as the chief priests of the famous dynasty of Kuru kings, particularly Tura Kavasheya, the *purohit* for king Janamejaya.[31] The Bhrigus, who were among those defeated by Sudas, appear as prominent teachers in later Vedic and Puranic lore as already noted. Such shifts would be impossible if Aryan and Dasyu were simply racial terms. Aryans and the Dasyus are not a racial or linguistic but a religious or spiritual divide, which changes along with human behavior.

Vedic battles are mainly among the Vedic people who are divided into various kingdoms, large and small, much as we find in the Mahabharata itself. Inimical peoples are generally Vedic Kshatriya or nobility among these five peoples. Divodasa, another great Vedic king of the Puru line, defeats Turvasha and Yadu in the Rig Veda.[32] A King named Divodasa in the Puranas defeats the Yadus. In the Mahabharata, Mandhata, a great Rig Vedic king and Dasyu conqueror, defeats the Druhyus, the lunar dynasty king of Gandhara or Afghanistan.[33] Parashurama, the sixth avatar of Lord Vishnu, chastises not only the Yadus

---

[28] Rig Veda VII.18, 6, 12, 13, 14
[29] Mahabharata Adi Parva 175-6
[30] Rig Veda VII.18.12
[31] Aitareya Brahmana viii.21
[32] Rig Veda IX.61.2
[33] Mahabharata Vanaparva 126.46

(Kartavirya Arjuna) but all the Kshatriyas. The great king of the solar dynasty Sagara also defeats the Yadus, who had allied themselves with many foreign peoples.

The main Vedic and Puranic battles are hence between the Purus and their allies (like the Ikshvakus) and the Yadus and their various allies (mainly the Turvashas but sometimes the Druhyus). This is similar to the Deva-Asura battle as it places the people of the Sarasvati in the north versus those in the southwest, but again as a battle between kindred peoples. In the Rig Veda Indra first makes Turvasha and Yadu great and then humbles them before the Purus.

Rama, the seventh avatar, defeats Ravana who is said to have been a Brahmin descendant of the rishi as well as a Rakshasa (demon). Rama's brother Shatrughna defeats Ravana's friend Lavana in Mathura,[34] the region of the Yadus, who is also said to be a Rakshasa. This connection between Lavana and Ravana suggests that Ravana himself was a Yadu, a Gujarati migrant to Sri Lanka, not a Dravidian. The first wave of Aryans to come to Sri Lanka were from Gujarat and hence Yadus. In this regard Ravana abducts Sita on the Godavari river, which was also in the region of the Yadus. Meanwhile Rama's other brother Bharata conquers Gandhara, the land of the Druhyus.

The Pandavas, with Krishna, the eighth avatar, defeat their own kinsmen, the Kauravas, who are said to be the incarnation of various demons,[35] on whose side are the Pandavas own gurus like Bhishma and Drona whom they must also kill. The Kauravas moreover are descendants of a Gandhara or Druhyu mother, Gandhari. Krishna also kills Kansa, a wicked Yadu king of his own family.

Other prominent instances occur when Brahmins are the enemies or the seers fight among themselves. Vritra, the enemy of Indra, the greatest Vedic God, is said in the Brahmanas and Puranas to have been a Brahmin and Indra has to atone for the

---

[34] Ramayana Uttara Kanda 70
[35] Mahabharata Adi Parva 67

sin of killing a Brahmin after killing him. This idea goes back to the Vedas where Vritra is the son of Tvashtar, one of the Vedic Gods and the patron deity of the sacrifice. Many of the conflicts in the Puranas are between the seers Vasishtha and Vishvamitra, both of which are honored throughout the literature of India as great seers. This conflict goes back to the time of Sudas where both vied to become his *purohita* or chief priest.

Vedic texts like the Brahmanas style the Dasyus as the fallen descendants of the Vedic king Vishvamitra, his older sons,[36] making them the older descendants of Vedic kings and seers. This reminds one of the story of Yayati wherein it was Puru, the youngest son, who inherited his kingdom, and his older sons Yadu and Turvasha who became inimical.

Mleccha, another term which later referred to people speaking a different language or to foreigners, was first used in the Sutra literature, Brahmanas and Mahabharata for people of western India from Gujarat to Punjab (realms of Anu, Druhyu and Yadu predominance) which had temporarily become a region of impure practices.[37] Such people were obviously speakers of Indo-European languages and were part of the same culture. These same regions included the kingdom of Sri Krishna in Dwaraka and the famous city of Takshashila in Gandhara from which the great grammarian Panini derived, which shows that such a designation was only temporary.

That the Vedic people must exclude those of different ethnic features or speaking non-Indo-European languages is an assumption deriving from the Aryan invasion theory and its Aryan race/language corollary. Vedic India was probably a pluralistic culture, like the pluralistic Vedic pantheon. The Vedas are the only books surviving from this era. This, however, does not mean that other books or teachings did not exist, including those in other languages. It may well be that the five Vedic peoples included groups who spoke different, even non-Indo-European languages,

---

[36] Aitareya Brahmana VII.18
[37] For example, Baudhayana Dharmasutra I.1.2, 14-15

or belonged to different ethnic groups or different races. There were other Aryan traditions deriving from or alternative to the Vedic like the Zoroastrian, or the Shramana traditions that gave birth to Buddhism and Jainism. Once the Aryan invasion idea is given up we must recognize the diversity of Vedic and Aryan culture. There is no need to stereotype it by race, language or even religion, particularly when the tradition that came from it is itself very diverse.

The Puranas make the Dravidians descendants of the Vedic family of Turvasha, one of the older Vedic peoples. These ancient historians did not feel any need to limit the Vedic people to one linguistic group. The Vedas portray the large region of north India which must have been as complex culturally then as today. In fact the Puranas regard the Chinese, Persians and other non-Indic peoples to be descendants of Vedic kings. The Vedas see all human beings as descendants of Manu, their legendary first man. The Vedic seers are said to generate not only human beings but the animal creation as well as the realms of the gods and the demons.

We can compare the Vedic wars with those of Europe. However fierce such battles were they were like the conflicts between the Catholics and Protestants or between the Germans and the French, that is, struggles between related peoples and religions, who also had long periods of peace between them besides the more dramatic periods of conflict. We don't have to bring in the idea of outside invaders to explain these conflicts and certainly Vedic and Puranic literature does not support this.

16. The Aryan/Dravidian Divide

The languages of South India are Dravidian, which is a different linguistic group than the Indo-European languages of North India. The two groups of languages have many different root words (though a number in common we might add), and above all a different grammatical structure, — the Dravidian being agglutinative and the Indo-European being inflected.

Dravidian languages possess a very old history of their own, which their legends, the Tamil Sangha literature, show a history in South India and Sri Lanka dating back over five thousand years.

Along with the difference of language there is a difference of skin color from north to south of India, with the southerners being darker in skin color (though northerners are hardly light in color by Western standards, with the exception of some people of the far northwest). Though a less pronounced difference than that of language it has been lumped together along with it again assuming that race and language must be the same.

The Aryan invasion theory has been used to explain both the linguistic and racial differences between the peoples of North and South India, and such differences have been put forth as "proof" of the invasion (as if no other explanation were possible). As the Aryans were made into a race, so were the Dravidians and the Aryan/Dravidian divide was turned into a racial war, the Aryan invaders versus the indigenous Dravidians of Harappa and Mohenjodaro. By this view the Vedic people promoted the superiority of their race and language and simply drove away those of different races or languages. We have already discussed how Sanskrit Aryan is never a racial term but a title of respect. Even the Dravidian kings called themselves Aryan. Nor is there anything in Vedic literature that places the Dravidians outside of the greater Vedic culture and ancestry. Hence to place Aryan against Dravidian as terms is itself a misuse of language. Be that as it may, the Aryan and Dravidian divide has also failed to prove itself.

Now it has been determined that scientifically speaking there is no such thing as Aryan and Dravidian races. The so-called Aryans and Dravidian races of India are members of the same Mediterranean branch of the Caucasian race, which prevailed in the ancient civilizations of Egypt and Sumeria and is still the main group in the Mediterranean area, North Africa, and the Middle East. The Caucasian race is not simply white but also contains dark-skinned types. Skin color and race is another nineteenth century idea that has been recently discarded.

Darker skin color is commonly found in peoples living in more southern regions and appears as an adjustment mechanism to hotter climates and greater sunshine. For example, southern Europeans are darker in skin color than northern Europeans, though they are not a different race because of this. This suggests that the Dravidian branch of the Mediterranean race must have lived in South India for some thousands of years to make this adjustment, and the same thing could be said of the people of North India as well if we would make them originally light-skinned invaders from the north.

The issue of language is similarly more complex. It is now known that Dravidian languages, with their agglutinative patterns, share common traits and are of the same broad linguistic group as such Asian and East European languages as Finnish, Hungarian, old Bulgarian, Turkish, Mongolian and Japanese, the Finno-Ugric and Ural-Altaic branches of languages. As the common point between these groups lies in Central Asia some scholars have recently proposed that the Dravidian peoples originally came from this region.

The same linguistic speculation that led to the Aryan invasion theory has, following the same logic, required a "Dravidian invasion." Not only are the Dravidians like the Aryans styled, invaders into India, they took the same route as the Aryans. The city-state of Elam in southwest Iran, east of Sumeria, which had a high civilization throughout the ancient period, shows an agglutinative structure like the Dravidian, as does possibly the Sumerian itself. This would place Dravidian type languages in Iran as well. Thereby the Dravidians, just like the Aryans, would have migrated (again the reason for which is not clear) from Central Asia and into Iran, with one group moving west to Mesopotamia and the other, apparently larger group, going east into India. Later the invading Aryans are said to have forced the Dravidians to move to the south of the country from their original homeland on the Indus and Sarasvati rivers. (However, we have already noted that there is no evidence of such migrations, nor of any Dravidian references to the Sarasvati like those of the Vedas.)

The Dravidian and Aryan invasion theories turn the migration of particular language/racial groups from Central Asia into a kind of panacea to explain the developments of race and language for much of humanity, particularly for India. However, both invasion theories appear far too simplistic given the complex ways in which cultures, languages and races move and interact.

The Dravidian claim to be indigenous to India has, like the Aryan, been discredited by linguistic argument. Yet the argument brings the Aryans and Dravidians back into contact with each other and derives them from the same region, suggesting a long term association between them outside of India. However, if we give up the invasion model such association can be better, explained by contact within India which we know was an historical fact.

Certainly the present population of India — which even the ancient Greeks and Persians regarded as dark-skinned — was not produced by light-skinned people from Central Asia (whether Aryan or Dravidian). Moreover, there cannot be a Dravidian invasion changing the language but not the population of India just like the Aryan invasion, as the idea is far-fetched to happen once but to happen twice in a row in the same region and by the same route is ridiculous.

If both the Aryan and Dravidian languages of India have affinities with those of Central Asia, and to peoples of different ethnic groups (the Indo-Aryan with the lighter skinned Europeans and the Dravidians with both light-skinned Finns and Hungarians, and Mongolian race Turks) a phenomenon is created that is too complex to be explained by mere migration alone. It takes languages across the racial boundaries that migration theories uphold and places them on par with other cultural affinities (like art or religion), which are not limited by race.

The linguistic divide between Aryan and Dravidian, as that between the Indo-European and other language groups, is also now being questioned. A greater Nostratic family of languages has been proposed that includes Indo-European, Dravidian and Semitic languages and looks for a common ancestor for all three. This requires a greater degree of contact between these groups which remote Central Asia cannot afford. Moreover, there are affinities between Sanskrit and the Munda or aboriginal languages of India, as S. Kalyanaraman has noted, that indicate a long and early contact, if not common evolution, which could have only happened in India. Such Vedic scholars as Sri Aurobindo have stated that the Dravidian and Sanskritic languages have much more in common than has yet been admitted and appear to have a common ancestor.

Dravidian history does not contradict Vedic history either. It credits the invention of the Tamil language, the oldest Dravidian tongue, to the rishi Agastya, one of the most prominent sages in the Rig Veda. Dravidian kings historically have called themselves Aryans and trace their descent through Manu (who in the Matsya Purāṇa is regarded as originally a south Indian king). Apart from language, moreover, both north and south India share a common religion and culture. Prior to Vedic Sanskrit there may have been a language that was the basis of both the Dravidian and Sanskritic languages in India.

The idea that the same culture cannot produce two different language systems may itself be questionable. It may have been the very power of Vedic culture and its sages, with their mastery of the word, that they could have produced not only Indo-European like languages but also Dravidian.

In any case, the Aryan/Dravidian divide is no longer sufficient to uphold the Aryan invasion theory. It leads to a more difficult to maintain Dravidian invasion theory. The Dravidian invasion theory is just a shadow cast by the Aryan invasion theory and reveals the erroneous nature of the latter.

Other aspects of the Aryan/Dravidian divide are predicated upon the invasion theory. For example, the idea that South India represents a pre-Vedic Shaivite culture as opposed to the Brahmanical culture of the North follows only from this. Otherwise we see Shaivism in the North, in Kailas, Benares and Kashmir, and Shiva as Rudra of the Vedas. What have thereby been proposed as radical differences between the North and South of India are merely regional variations in the vast cultural complex of the big country and its interrelated spiritual traditions.

Dravidian pride or nationalism need not depend upon the Aryan invasion theory or denigrating the culture of North India. The Dravidians have long been one of the most important peoples of India and, perhaps ironically, have been the best preservers of Vedic culture itself. The best Vedic Sanskrit, rituals and traditions can be found only in the South of India. That South India was able to do this suggests the importance and antiquity of Vedic culture to this region.

17. Vedic Kings and Empires

Vedic texts like Shatapatha and Aitareya Brahmanas list a group of ten to sixteen kings, including a number of figures of the Rig Veda like Sudas, as having conquered the region of India from "sea to sea".[38] Lands of the Vedic people are mentioned in these texts from Gandhara (Afghanistan) in the west to Videha (Bihar) in the east, and south to Vidarbha (Maharashtra), as well as from the western to the eastern oceans. The lands mentioned in the Vedas are much vaster in scope than those in any other ancient literature. The Vedas are hardly the pronouncements of a limited local culture or new intruders who had not yet known the region. They speak of a region equivalent to the region of Europe from the Baltic to the Mediterranean seas and from Spain to Poland.

These passages were ignored by nineteenth century scholars

---

[38] Aitareya Brahmana VIII.21-23; Shatapatha Brahmana XIII.5.4.

dominated by the invasion theory, who stated that the Vedas show no evidence of large empires in India. The main reason again was the so-called absence of archaeological data. However, the Harappan culture, which now has sites in most of these regions mentioned in the Brahmanas, should cause us to take these references seriously. Were these figures great kings or emperors of the Harappan (Sarasvati) culture? Surely such a large culture would have maintained some memory of its great kings.

18. Vedic Astronomical Lore

Vedic texts contain interesting astronomical lore. The Vedic calendar was based upon astronomical sightings of the equinoxes and solstices which change periodically owing to the precession of the earth on its axis. Such texts as Vedanga Jyotish[39] speak of a time when the vernal equinox was in the middle of the constellation (*Nakshatra*) Aslesha (a point about 23 degrees 20 minutes Cancer). This would have occurred around 1400 BC. Many Brahmanas, and the Yajur and Atharva Vedas speak of the vernal equinox in the Krittikas (Pleiades; early Taurus) and the summer solstice (*ayana*) in Magha (early Leo).[40] This yields a date of around 2500 BC. Yet earlier astronomical eras than these are mentioned but these two have numerous references to substantiate them. They prove that the Vedic culture existed at the time of the Harappan culture and already had a sophisticated system of astronomy.

Such references were merely ignored or pronounced unintelligible by Western scholars because they yielded too early a date for the Vedas than what was presumed, not because such references did not exist. One point raised by Western scholars was that there was nothing archaeological to substantiate such positions as the dates reveal. Now we see there is indeed that ar-

---

[39] *Vedanga Jyotish of Lagadha* (New Delhi, India: Indian National Science Academy, 1985), pp.12-13.

[40] For example, Atharva Veda XIX.7.2.

chaeological evidence through the Harappan or Sarasvati civilization.

Had such astronomical references been found in ancient Greek texts, we might add, they would have been hailed as great scientific achievements, among the greatest of ancient humanity. It is only because they occurred in Hindu texts that they have not been given proper credit. On the contrary, we are told that the Hindus were unscientific, which has been an excuse to ignore the scientific achievements mentioned in the Vedas.

Recently Subhash Kak has also discovered an astronomical code in the structure of the Rig Veda that shows a knowledge of the periods of the planets, as well as reflecting a location for the hymns around 22 degrees north, or the point where the Sarasvati used to enter the ocean.[41]

19. Painted Grey Ware

One of the more recent archaeological ideas is that the Vedic culture is evidenced by Painted Grey Ware pottery in North India, which appears to date around 1000 BC and was found in the same region between the Ganges and Yamuna as later Vedic culture is related to. It is thought to be an inferior grade of pottery and to be associated with the use of iron that the Vedas are thought to mention. However, it is associated with a pig and rice culture, not the cow and barley culture of the Vedas. Moreover, it is now found to be an organic development of indigenous pottery, not an introduction of invaders.

Painted Grey Ware culture represents an indigenous cultural development and does not reflect any cultural intrusion from the West, that is, an Indo-Aryan invasion. Therefore, there is no archaeological evidence corroborating the fact of an Indo-Aryan invasion.[42]

---

[41] Subhash Kak, "The Astronomical Code of the Rig Veda", *Current Science* Vol.66, No.4, 25 February 1994., pp.323-326.

[42] J. Shaffer, "The Indo-Aryan Invasions: Cultural Myth and Archaeological Reality", from J. Lukacs Ed., *The People of South Asia* (New York: Plenum, 1984), p.85.

Painted Grey Ware is associated with sites that occur after the drying up of the Sarasvati river, which further indicates its post-Vedic nature.

20. Aryans in the Ancient Middle East

In addition, the Aryans in the Middle East, most notably the Hittites, have now been found to have been in that region at least as early as 2200 BC, wherein they are already mentioned in Sumerian literature. In fact, they derived their script from that of the third dynasty of Sumeria. Any Aryan invasion into the Middle East has been pushed back some centuries, though the evidence so far is that the people of the mountain regions of the Middle East were Indo-Europeans as far as recorded history can be traced.

The Indo-European Kassites of the ancient Middle East worshipped Vedic Gods like Surya and the Maruts, as well as one named Himalaya. The Hittites and Mittani signed a treaty with the name of the Vedic Gods — Indra, Mitra, Varuna and Nasatyas — around 1400 BC. The Hittites have a treatise on chariot racing written in almost pure Sanskrit. The Indo-Europeans of the ancient Middle East spoke Indo-Aryan, not Indo-Iranian languages and thereby show a Vedic culture in that region of the world as well.[43] This shows that Vedic culture extended from India to Anatolia by 2000 BC.

When the Linear B of the Minoan Script, dating from 1500-1100 BC, was deciphered it proved to be an earlier form of the Greek language. This has pushed the Greek presence in Greece back to 2000 or even 3000 BC, changing the Aryan entrance into this region back many centuries. It may well be that the early Minoan culture spoke a Greek or Indo-European language.

As there is no longer any invasion of Aryan peoples into Greece and the Middle East around 1500 BC, and as their presence in the region must be pushed back probably a thousand

---

[43] T. Burrow, "The Proto-Indoaryans", *Journal of the Royal Asiatic Society,* No. 2, 1973, pp.123-140.

*years or more, there is no necessity to make an Aryan invasion
of India at this time to coincide along with it.* On the contrary,
if the Aryan entrance into these regions must be pushed back, so
must their entry into India.

21. Indus Writing

The Indus Valley culture had a form of writing, evidenced
by numerous seals found in the ruins. On the assumption of the
Aryan invasion it was assumed to be non-Vedic and probably
Dravidian, though this was never proved. Now it has been shown
that the majority of the late Indus signs are identical with those
of early Brahmi, the oldest Sanskritic script, and that there is an
organic development between the two scripts. The scripts show
a continuity which suggests that they reflect the same language
and culture.

Prevalent models, primarily the work of Subhash Kak, show
an Indo-European basis for that language.[44] This is based on a
discovery that the script uses a genitive (possessive) case, which
is typical of Indo-European but not Dravidian languages. However, there are not yet long enough inscriptions to guarantee a
proper decipherment. Based upon the location of the culture
Subhash Kak is suggesting that the script be renamed "Sarasvati
script."

22. Sanskrit

According to proponents of the Aryan invasion theory the
only thing that really marks the Aryans is their language. No
other specific cultural trait or artefact can be clearly related to

---

[44] See G.R. Hunter, *The Script of Harappa and Mohenjodaro and Its Con-
nection with Other Scripts* (London: Kegan Paul, Trench, Trubner & Co.,
1934). Also see J.E. Mitchiner, *Studies in the Indus Valley Inscriptions* (New
Delhi, India: Oxford and IBH, 1978). Note particularly the work of Subhash
Kak as in "A Frequency Analysis of the Indus Script", *Cryptologia,* July 1988,
Volume XII, Number 3; "Indus Writing", *The Mankind Quarterly,* Volume 30,
Nos. 1 & 2, Fall/Winter 1989; and "On the Decipherment of the Indus Script
— A Preliminary Study of its Connection with Brahmi", *Indian Journal of
History of Science,* 22(1):51-62 (1987).

them. Yet even here we have a paradox. Sanskrit is supposed to be the language of primitive invaders and yet it is, by the opinion of many, one of it not the most refined language in the world. It has been regarded as the best language for computers because of its clarity. It is also a highly self-contained language developing organically out of specific roots, quite unlike English which is a mixture of various different languages like old German, Danish and French, with an admixture of Greek and Latin, reflecting a land that was invaded by many different peoples.

Moreover, Sanskrit is a highly musical and metrical language. It possesses the oldest and most sophisticated grammatical science, going back to a period before the Buddha to the time of Panini and before, as he mentions several older grammatical traditions, some of which can be found in Vedic texts. Even the oldest Sanskrit, that of the Rig Veda, is done in complex meters and filled with various sophisticated plays on the sounds of words. It is a language filled with synonyms indicating a long and rich development. Above all it has an entire mysticism of sound, mantra and the Divine Word.

In other words, Sanskrit does not appear as the legacy of barbarian hordes but that of an old, venerable, sophisticated poetic culture. Such a language requires a culture to produce it. This refined language fits quite well with the refined culture of Harappa but not with that of the Aryan invasion.

23. Indian Civilization, an Indigenous Development

Under the idea that all civilization came from the Middle East, it assumed that Harappan culture derived its impetus from the Middle East, probably Sumeria. Recent French excavations have shown that all the antecedents of the Indus culture can be found within India going back before 6500 BC as revealed by the Mehrgarh site near the Bolan Pass in Pakistan. Mehrgarh is the largest village/town culture of its period anywhere in the world and develops into the Indus culture by a series of stages, showing the evolution of agriculture and arts and crafts typical of Harappa.[45]

In short, Western scholars are also beginning to reject the Aryan invasion or any outside origin for Hindu civilization:

> Current archaeological data do not support the exist-
> ence of an Indo-Aryan or European invasion into South
> Asia at any time in the pre- or protohistoric periods. In-
> stead, it is possible to document archaeologically a series
> of cultural changes reflecting indigenous cultural develop-
> ment from prehistoric to historic periods.
>
> The Indo-Aryan invasion as an academic concept in
> eighteenth and nineteenth century Europe reflected the
> cultural milieu of the period. Linguistic data were used to
> validate the concept that in turn was used to interpret ar-
> chaeological and anthropological data.[46]

The idea of the Aryan invasion was the product of linguistic speculation and archaeological data was twisted into that model. Now the archaeological data is shown either not to fit the theory or the date ascribed to it, while the literary evidence (the Vedas) never did. Even scholars who are still postulating a common Aryan homeland in Europe or Central Asia are making the pe-riod of diffusion from it from 4000 to 6000 BC, or early enough to allow an entry of Indo-Aryans into India before the beginning of the Harappan culture.

Colin Renfrew, places the Indo-Europeans in Greece as early as 6000 BC. He suggests such a possible early date for their entry into India as well:

> As far as I can see there is nothing in the Hymns of the
> Rig Veda which demonstrates that the Vedic-speaking
> population were intrusive to the area: this comes rather

---

[45] J.F. Jarrige and R.H. Meadow, "The Antecedents of Civilization in the Indus Valley", *Scientific American,* August, 1980.

[46] J. Shaffer, "The Indo-Aryan Invasions: Cultural Myth and Archaeological Reality", from J. Lukacs Ed., *The People of South Asia* (New York: Plenum, 1984), p.88.

from a historical assumption of the "coming of the Indo-European."[47]

When Wheeler speaks of "the Aryan invasion of the Land of the Seven Rivers, the Punjab," he has no warranty at all, so far as I can see. If one checks the dozen references in the Rig Veda to the Seven Rivers, there is nothing in them that to me implies an invasion: the land of the Seven Rivers is the land of the Rig Veda, the scene of action.[48]

Despite Wheeler's comments, it is difficult to see what is particularly non-Aryan about the Indus Valley civilization.[49]

Renfrew suggests that the Indus Valley civilization was in fact Indo-Aryan:

> This hypothesis that early Indo-European languages were spoken in north India with Pakistan and on the Iranian plateau at the sixth millennium BC has the merit of harmonizing symmetrically with the theory for the origin of the Indo-European languages in Europe. It also emphasizes the continuity in the Indus Valley and adjacent areas from the early neolithic through to the floruit of the Indus Valley civilization.[50]

In addition, it does not mean that the Rig Veda dates from the Harappan era. Harappan culture resembles that of the Yajur Veda and the Brahmanas, or the later Vedic era. If anything the Rig Veda appears to reflect the pre-Indus period in India, when the Sarasvati river was more prominent.

---

[47] C. Renfrew, *Archeology and Language* (New York: Cambridge University Press, 1987), pp.182.

[48] Ibid., p.188.

[49] Ibid., p.190.

[50] Ibid., p.196.

24. The New Model

The New Model of ancient India that has emerged from the collapse of the Aryan invasion theory is that of an indigenous development of civilization in ancient India from the Mehrgarh site of 6500 BC. The people in this tradition are the same basic ethnic groups as in India today, with their same basic types of languages — Indo-European and Dravidian. There is a progressive process of the domestication of animals, particularly cattle, the development of agriculture, beginning with barley and then later wheat and rice, and the use of metal, beginning with copper and culminating in iron, along with the development of villages and towns. Later Harappan (Sarasvati) civilization 3100-1900 BC show massive cities, complex agriculture and metallurgy, sophistication of arts and crafts, and precision in weights and measures. This Sarasvati civilization was a center of trading and for the diffusion of civilization throughout South and West Asia, which often dominated the Mesopotamian region.

Post-Harappan civilization 1900-1000 BC shows the abandonment of the Harappan towns owing to ecological and river changes but without a real break in the continuity of the culture. There is a decentralization and relocation in which the same basic agricultural and artistic traditions continue, along with a few significant urban sites like Dwaraka. This gradually develops into the Gangetic civilization of the first millennium BC, which is the classical civilization of ancient India, which retains its memory of its origin in the Sarasvati region through the Vedas.

The layers of Vedic literature fit in perfectly well with this sequence:

1. 6500-3100 BC, Pre-Harappan, early Rig Vedic
2. 3100-1900 BC, Mature Harappan 3100-1900, period of the Four Vedas
3. 1900-1000 BC, Late Harappan, late Vedic and Brahmana period

The sequence of development in the literature does not parallel a migration into India but the historical development of civilization in India from the Sarasvati to the Ganges.

25. Ancient History Revised

We have examined the Aryan invasion theory and seen how it has continually failed to prove itself. It has tried to readjust itself to new evidence that has gradually undermined it and now leaves nothing left to hold it up. Therefore we must look at the history of India and the world in the light of the collapse of the invasion theory. The acceptance of a Vedic nature to Harappan and pre-Harappan civilization creates a revolution in our view of history, not just of India but of the entire world.

First, it equates Indo-European peoples with one of the largest and oldest ancient civilizations not in Europe or the Middle East but in South Asia. The idea that the Indo-Europeans were originally nomads or primitive in culture and took over civilization from the peoples of the Middle East is thereby called into question. The Indo-Europeans appear as early and independent inventors of civilization of a sophisticated urban basis by the third millennium BC. This suggests a greater antiquity and sophistication for other Indo-European cultures, those of Europe, the Middle East and Central Asia. The origins of European culture may lie not with the ancient Greeks but with the Hindus and be found in the Vedas, not as the record of nomadic Indo-European culture but of early Indo-European urban civilization.

Second, it turns the ancient Vedas of India into an authentic record of a culture at least as old as the third millennium BC. As the Vedic literary record is very large, it indicates that we retain a priceless treasure, a well preserved literary record from our ancient ancestors over four thousand years old, complete with accents and commentaries. The Vedas are chanted by Brahmins today much as they were over four thousand years ago in the Indus-Sarasvati culture. We could only compare this to the condition if ancient Egyptian teachings were still being chanted today in modern Egypt. This means that the Vedas should be examined by all people who wish to truly understand ancient humanity. It requires a reexamination of the Vedas and taking their statements seriously when they speak of the vastness and sophisticated nature of their culture.

Third, it makes Vedic India perhaps the oldest, largest and most central of the world's cultures. Some have proposed that the Harappan culture is the oldest in the world because of its size and uniformity. That this culture was able to preserve its continuity would add much weight to the argument. This would require that we must reexamine Vedic India to understand the root of civilization from which we have developed, or perhaps fallen.

In this regard the great Dravidian and Munda (aboriginal) connections inherent in the Vedas and in ancient India need to be examined. Not only does this reinterpretation of the Vedas push Indo-European civilization back further, it also breaks down the divide between Indo-European and other cultures. Vedic literature may therefore allow us to link up many ancient cultures and see the greater commonality of ancient civilization.

Fourth, it indicates that traditional literature and ancient calendars all over the world have to be taken more seriously, not only Hindu but Chinese, Mayan and others. It shows that the ancients are not as bad historians as we have thought, but that we are bad interpreters of their literature. It would require a totally different look at the ancient world.

26. Political and Social Ramifications

In closing, it is important to examine the social and political implications of the Aryan invasion idea:

First, it served to divide India into a northern Aryan and southern Dravidian culture which were made hostile to each other. This kept the Hindus divided and is still a source of social tension. It created the ideas of an Aryan and a Dravidian "race" in India as two distinct entities, even though there never was any real scientific basis for this idea.

Second, it gave the British an excuse for their conquest of India. They could claim to be doing only what the Aryan ancestors of the Hindus had previously done millennia ago. This same justification could be used by the Muslims or any other invaders of India.

Third, it served to make Vedic culture later than and possibly derived from the Middle Eastern. It made the ancient civilization of India fragmented, with the Harappan culture mysteriously disappearing without a trace, making the development of civilization in India appear broken. With the proximity and relationship of Middle Eastern civilization with the Bible and Christianity, this kept the Hindu religion as a sidelight to the development of religion and civilization in the West.

Fourth, it allowed the sciences of India to be given a Greek basis, as any Vedic basis for sciences like astronomy was largely disqualified by the primitive nature of the Vedic culture (even though the Vedas commonly mention sophisticated mathematical and astronomical data). This served to make Indian culture subservient to that of Greece and Europe.

Fifth, it gave the Marxists a good basis for projecting their class struggle model of society on to India, with the invading Brahmins oppressing the indigenous Shudras (lower castes). Even today the invasion theory is used to inflame the sentiments of the backward classes in India against the Brahmins who, by this idea, originally invaded India and conquered and enslaved the indigenous population and turned them into Shudras.

The Aryan invasion theory discredited not only the Vedas, but the genealogies of the Puranas, and their long lists of kings before the Buddha or Krishna were left without any historical basis (or somehow turned into pre-Vedic or non-Aryan people). The Mahabharata, instead of a civil war in which all the main kings of India participated as it is described, became a local skirmish among petty princes that was later exaggerated by poets. In short, the Aryan invasion theory discredited the most of the Hindu tradition and almost all its ancient literature. It turned its scriptures and sages into fantasies and exaggerations.

This served a social, political and economic purpose of domination, proving the superiority of Western culture, religion, or political systems and the Aryan invasion theory was often quoted for this purpose. It makes Hindus feel that their culture is not the great thing that their sages and ancestors had said it was. It causes them to feel ashamed of their culture — that its basis is neither historical nor scientific but only imaginary, while being actually rooted in invasion and oppression. It makes them feel that the main line of civilization was developed first in the Middle East and then in Europe and that the culture of India is peripheral and secondary to the real development of world culture. Such a view does not appear to be good scholarship or archaeological proof but only cultural imperialism. Western Vedic scholars did in the intellectual sphere what the British army did in the political realm — discredit, divide and conquer the Hindus.

Unfortunately, those challenging the theory, even on the most objective archaeological grounds like the rediscovery of the Sarasvati river, have been accused of political motives, often by the very groups who have been using the invasion theory for their own political advantage, like Marxist thinkers in India. Those rejecting the Aryan invasion may even be called "communal" for bringing out evidence that may give pride to the majority community in India.

In short, the compelling reasons for the Aryan invasion theory were neither literary nor archaeological but political and religious — that is to say, not scholarship but prejudice. Such prejudice may not have been intentional but deep-seated political and religious views easily cloud and blur our thinking. We are only now learning to examine our cultural prejudices in looking at the world. This is one of the great necessities of the global era. That nineteenth century views of history may be as biased or out of date as nineteenth century views of science or politics should not surprise us.

What has happened in India, the misinterpretation of its ancient history and a new move to restore validity to it, is reflected in much of the new archeology developing throughout the world, particularly when native people take up the task of interpreting their own history. The misinterpretation of the Vedas was part of a general inability to recognize ancient cultures outside of the Middle East (in fact many of these were also misinterpreted). We can expect new discoveries in other parts of the world showing a greater antiquity and sophistication to a number of cultures.

Unfortunately, the Eurocentric approach of the Aryan invasion theory has not been questioned more, particularly by Hindus. Strangely, even the anti-colonial Marxists have taken up this colonial view as their own. Even though Indian Vedic scholars like Dayananda Sarasvati, Tilak and Aurobindo rejected it, most Hindus today passively accept it. They allow Western, often Christian scholars to interpret their history for them and quite naturally Hinduism is kept in a reduced role. Many Hindus still accept, read or even honor the translations of the Vedas done by such nineteenth century Christian missionary scholars as Max Muller, Griffith, Monier-Williams and H.H. Wilson. Would modern Christians accept an interpretation of the Bible or Biblical history done by Hindus aimed at converting them to Hinduism? Universities in India still use these Western history books and Western Vedic translations that propound these views which denigrate their own culture and country.

The modern Western academic world is sensitive to criticisms of cultural and social biases. For scholars to take a stand against this biased interpretation of the Vedas would indeed cause a reexamination of many of these historical ideas which cannot stand objective scrutiny. But if Hindu scholars are silent or passively accept the misinterpretation of their culture, it will undoubtedly continue, and they will have no one to blame but themselves. It is not an issue to be taken lightly because how a culture is defined historically creates the perspective from which it is viewed in the modern social and intellectual context all over the world. Tolerance is not in allowing a false view of one's own culture and religion to be propagated without question. That is merely self-betrayal.